Blue Ribbon Techniques

Burning and Texturing Methods

by

William Veasey

Schiffer Publishing Ltd

Dedication

To all who have agonized over the detailing of
a bird carving.

Bill Veasey

This book may be purchased from the publisher.
Please include $1.50 postage.
Try your bookstore first.

Designed by Ellen J. Taylor

Published by Schiffer Publishing Ltd., 1469 Morstein Road, West Chester,
Pennsylvania 19380

Front cover carving by Sina "Pat" Kurman
Back cover carvings by Paul Suarez and Sina "Pat" Kurman
Photography by Tricia Veasey
Project preparation by:
        Debra Norvell
        William Veasey
        Dotty Veasey
        Roxayne Culley

Purpose: To acquaint beginning carvers with as wide a range as possible of accepted texturing methods and techniques so as to enable them to progress more quickly in this highly satisfying art form.

Acknowledgment

Acknowledgment of Ward Foundation for giving all of us the opportunity of going beyond where we thought we could go.

Bill Veasey

Burning and texturing used in bird carving are just like carving and painting—to learn how to burn one must burn—to learn how to texture one must texture and so on and so on and on and on and on.

One cannot ever practice enough. There are some things which once known may ease the way.

1. Be certain that you **see**. Many people do not see well—use good light and if you have a slight problem use magnifyers.

2. Do not try to use every technique in every carving—make your choices early on so there will be simplicity and continuity in your carving.

3. After knowledge and practice, your most important tool is your **pencil**. Use it—do not spare it—it is all important. If you do not have a road map it is hard if not impossible to follow.

4. Study fine carvings and photographs of the same.

5. Keep your burning pen sharp.

6. Do not use too much heat, some of the finest burning I have ever seen hardly discolors the wood—control is the key.

7. Paint will not cover up bad texturing—it will only make it stand out.

8. Do not be discouraged—remember that every one was at one time in their development right where you are now.

9. Experiment—reach out—go beyond where you are—that is growth.

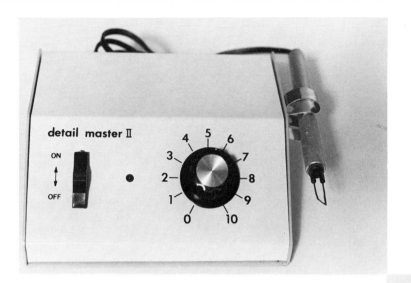

A. A sophisticated burner designed for use in bird carving is an essential tool. I recommend the Detail Master for two reasons; It was helpful in original design and it is a superior unit.

B. The Hot tool is a constant heat, strong, replaceable tip, burning pen with available reostat and multi-tip accessories—very useful in many applications (edging feathers, etc.). I suggest using this burner in addition to the more sophisticated units, not instead.

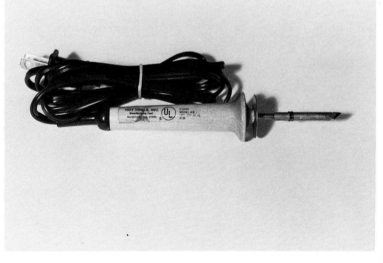

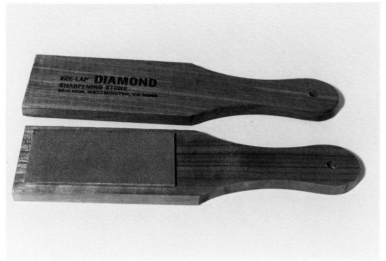

A. All burning tips must be sharpened occasionally, generally in direct proportion to the amount of use and the type of tip material (Note—learn your tip material). Oversharpening only wears out the tips faster. If carbon builds up on a unit with reostat, turn the heat up until it is red. This will generally burn off the carbon and eliminate the need for immediate sharpening.

Figure A represents an excellent sharpener. It is diamond coated steel, fine grit, and will sharpen tips cleanly and quickly.

B. A fine grit oil stone which will work just as well but will require a little more time. Another good method would be a leather strop coated with aluminum oxide (very fine) in an oil base.

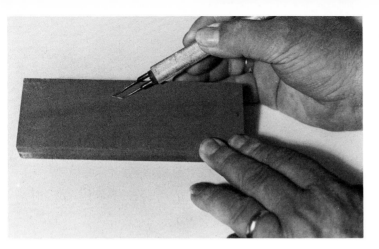

A. Examples of sharpening different tips on fine stone.

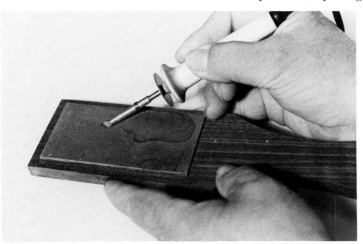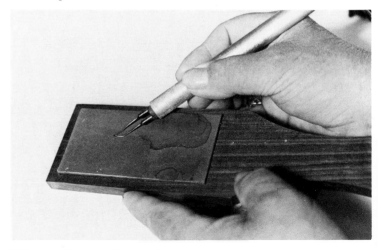

B. Examples of sharpening different tips on diamond stone.

A. & B. Examples of very fine completely burned sleeping Red Head hen. Take particular note of transitional areas (chest to sides) chest to head—sides to under rump, etc.

A. Detail of chest burning and transition to side.

B. Detail of head and transition to chest. Also note the wing area where the head is tucked.

A. Detail of chest straight on.

B. Detail of head and back.

A. Detail of transition of chest to sides.

B. Detail of side pockets and wing area. Note the random look in feather layout.

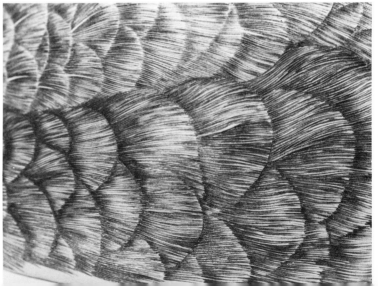

A. Detail of rump area.

B. Detail of rump and upper tail.

A. Detail of scapulars.

B. Detail of tertials and primaries.

A. Pintail head. Note directional flow of feathers.

B. Detail of cheeks and eye area.

C. Detail of crown.

D. Detail back of head area.

A. Example of coarse, deep burning in a straight line method.

B. Same head and method showing direction at back of head and through eye channel.

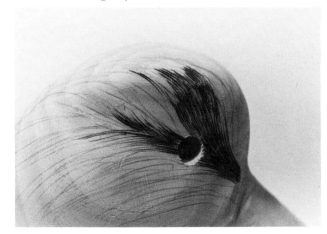

C. Example of giving an illusion of depth in the eye channel by using it as a line of demarcation. Flowing away from it on either side. Note an indent type of burn on the fore cheek which creates the illusion of pin feathers.

D. Another example of letter C.

A. Example of the cheek area of the wood duck drake.

B. Example of the crown area of the wood duck drake.

C. Example of the side of crest of the wood duck drake.

D. Example of the back of crest of the wood duck drake.

A. Layer type of indent burning to simulate pin feathers on cheek.

B. Example of loose feather pattern on crown.

C. Example of coarse, straight line burning.

D. Example of bill detail using a burner instead of carving.

Note—layering of feather groups on this page was done entirely by outlining with a burner instead of carving. Notice the crisp, neat, clean manner in which each feather stands out.

A. Detail of upper tail and tail coverts of a wood duck.

B. Upper tail and tertial area, raised and overlapped to accomodate inserted primaries.

C. Tail and primary area of a Red Head.

D. Under tail of wood duck.

A. Wood duck tertial and secondaries with coverts. Note the neat layering and angle of back showing pin shaft.

B. Tertial and coverts. Note the raised shafts and neatness.

A. Detail of hooded merganser. Note the tertials, coverts, and crossed primary feathers. Also note that the feathers are "carved" with a burning pen.

B. Tertial area of pintail drake.

A. Tail covert and primaries of pintail drake.

B. Primaries and tertials of pintail.

A. Tertial group with raised shafts on pintail.

B. Tertials and coverts of pintail.

A. Layout and direction of burn for tertials and secondaries of Canada Goose.

B. Secondaries and coverts of the Canada Goose. Note the layout of the side pockets.

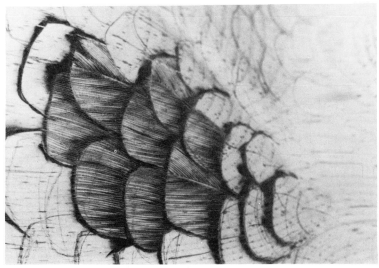

A. Feather group. Note the squarish feathers on the wing of the Canada Goose.

B. Example of edging feather groups.

C. Example of edging feather groups.

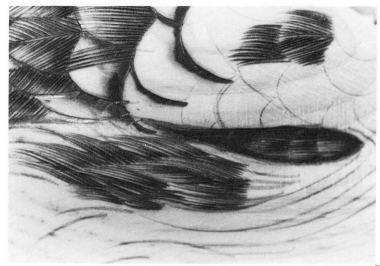

A. Layering and swirl type burning on the side pockets is particularly useful on most drakes where there is no discernable feather pattern.

B. Example of layer burning on the shoulder. Note the pencil layout—pencil is one of the most important tools, use it always.

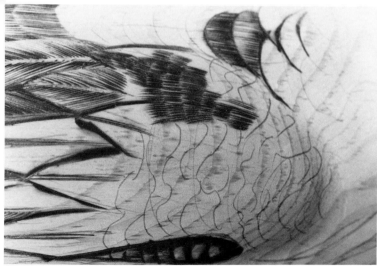

A. Example of feather group on wings.

B. Example of feather group on wings showing transition through fill area of the neck joint.

A. Layout of feathers growing on foreback of pintail. Note transition of some feathers showing shaft and others not— so that there will not be an abrupt stop and start.

B. Transition of rounded to pointed feathers.

A. Example of tertials and coverts.

B. Example of tertials, coverts, and secondaries.

C. Example of tertials, coverts, and primaries.

D. Example of tertials, coverts, secondaries, primaries, and rump.

A. Example of tertials, primaries, tail coverts, and tail.

B. Example of tertials, primaries, and secondaries.

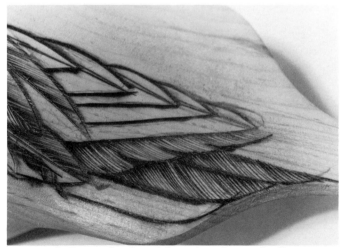

C. Example of tertials, primaries, and tail.

D. Example of tail and tail coverts.

A. Example of a side pocket indent and a wing area indent instead of outlining feathers, gives a softer edging by indenting point of burners deeper around the edge of feather forward of one being burned.

B. Example of indent type of burning on wing.

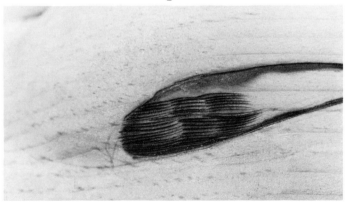

C. Small feather group on folded area of wing.

D. Example of the side pocket feather group of a Mallard hen.

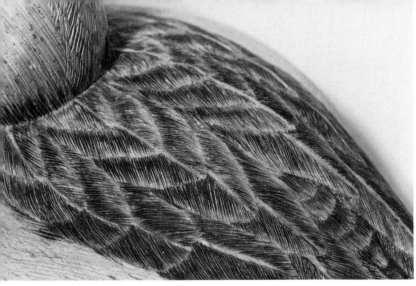

A. Back (wings) area of canvasback. Example of rolled feathers.

B. Example of layered feathers on rump, tertials and primaries.

C. Example of tertials, primaries and tail.

A. Example of tertials, primaries and rump area on the miniature Mallard.

B. Example of tertials, rump and tail area of miniature Mallard.

C. Example of first tracing of tail feather prior to layering with burner.

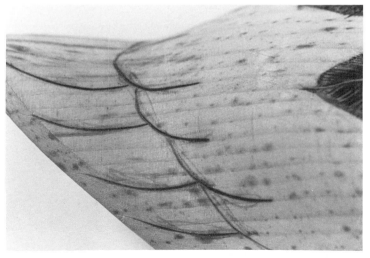

A. Example of the tertial area of the miniature Mallard with shafts not raised and arced barbs.

B. Example of the wing area and side pockets with example 7 raised shafts.

C. Example of side pockets, raised shafts and arced barbs.

D. Example of tertial area and tertial coverts.

A. Example of wing area, layered feathers, and raised shafts.

B. Example of the forward area of wing.

C. Example of the tail and tail coverts of a Mallard.

D. Example of the wing area with raised shafts and arced barbs.

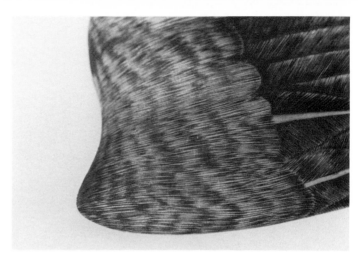

A. Example of extended wing (teal), tertials and secondaries.

B. Example of wing coverts done in a layered method.

C. Example of secondaries raised by burner instead of carved.

D. Example set of ten primary feathers for inserts into this wing.

A. Example of feather group common to Canada Goose—layered and burned.

B. Example of feather group common to Canada Goose—layered and burned. Note squarish feathers.

A. Example of the feather group of Pintail tertial.

B. Example of side pocket.

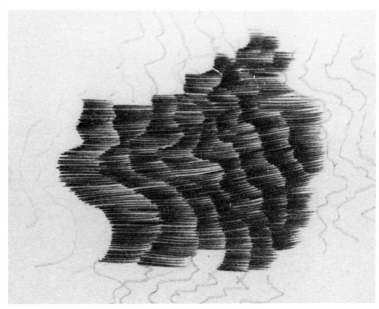

A. Example of layer type burn to simulate pin feather.

B. Example of feather group burns for crowns, rump, etc.

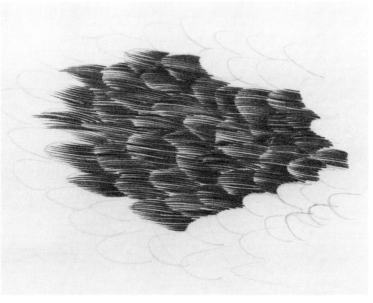

A. Layer and swirl with multi-tip of Hot tool.

B. Feather pattern with multi-tip of Hot tool.

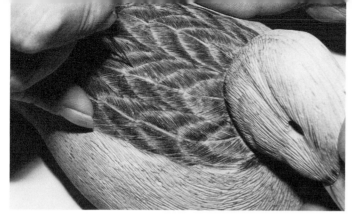

A. Burning rounded feathers. Note point of pen is placed at interior of feather with slight hesitation to burn slightly deeper.

B. Drawing blade of burner over broader area of feather to get more line from burn quicker.

C. Sometimes on rounded feathers you must turn the bird around and finish the barb stroke from an appropriate direction.

D. Again using extreme tip of pen to create layered effect without outlining feather. Gives a very soft effect.

A. Wing layout of teal hen outlined and partially burned.

B. Tertials and secondaries partially burned.

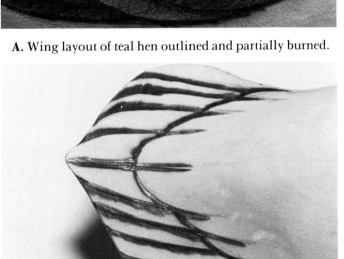

C. Tail of teal outlined.

D. Entire back (wings) of teal hen partially burned.

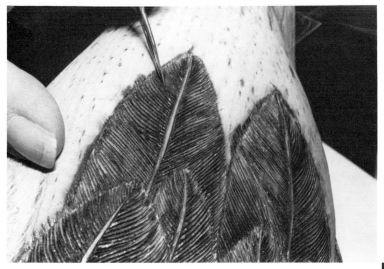

A. Broadening burn in barb figuration to simulate split in side feather.

B. Another split in tertial feather—do not over use split.

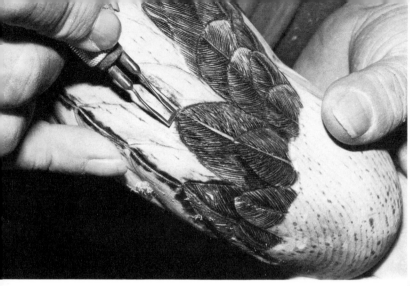

A. Use of square tip to raise feathers and quills.

B. Use of square tip to raise tail feathers and tail coverts.

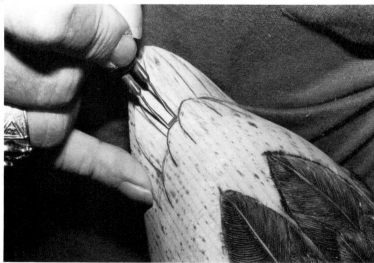

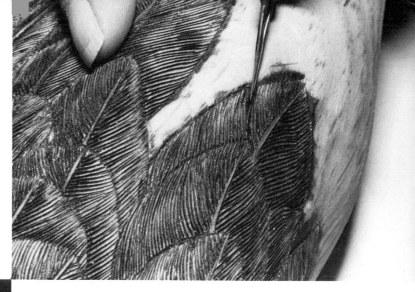

A. Using 45° tip to arc barbs on large feather.

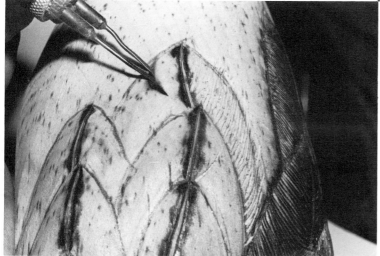

B. Burning split before barbs.

A. Carving split in pintail tertial with 45° burning pen.

B. Broadening same split.

A. Detailing cape area of pintail.

B. Detailing cape area of pintail.

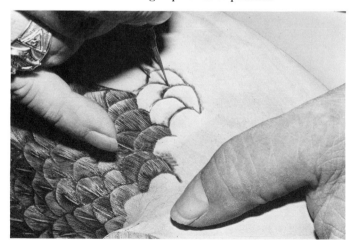

C. Wing area outlined.

D. Detailing tail of pintail.

A. Example of layered swirl pattern over stoned area.

B. Further example of layered swirl pattern.

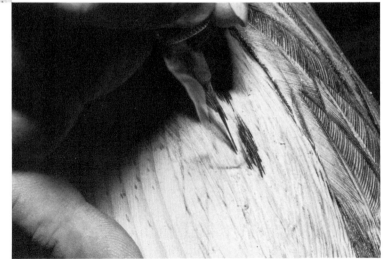

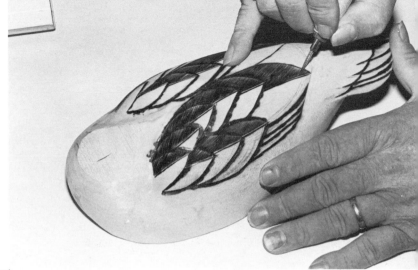

A. Example of burning large tertial feather. Note stability with little finger.

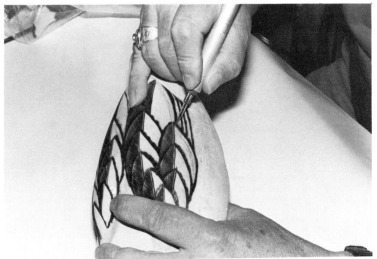

B. Example of burning barbs in secondaries.

A. Example of the cape area and wings of the wood duck.

B. Example of the tertial and secondary area of the wood duck.

C. Example of tertial overlay of the wood duck.

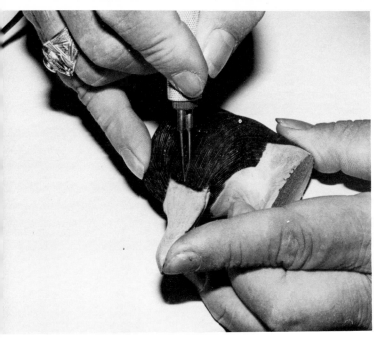

A. Example of straight line burning on a teal hen head.

B. Example of straight line burning on crown of teal hen head.

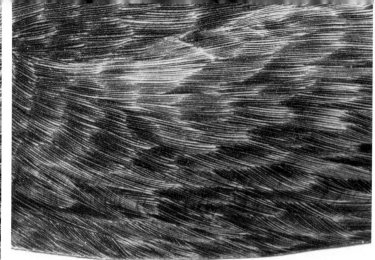

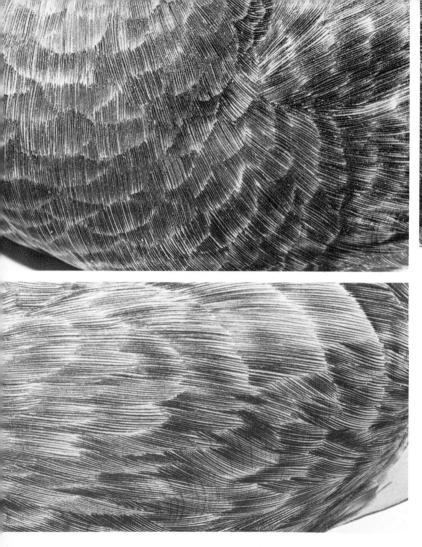

A. Example of chest layering and transitional burn on wood duck drake.

B. Example of side random layer in wood duck drake.

C. Example of side of wood duck drake. Note at top rear (right) the transition into regular pattern to create black and white slashes on side pockets of wood duck drake.

A. Example of the chest of the wood duck drake using indent type of burn (no definite outline).

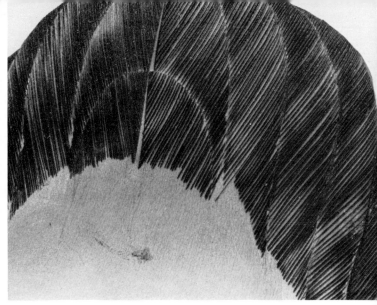

B. Example of the tail layout of the wood duck drake.

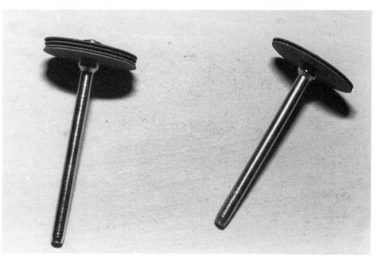

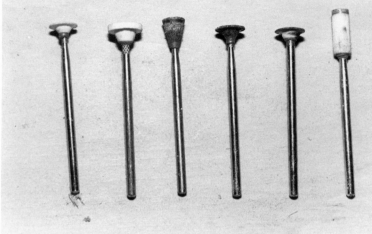

A. For other types of texturing dental separating discs may be used in multiples with separator.

B. Examples of various stones used for fine texturing.

C. Worn down dental discs for tight places.

D. Solid rasp used for banging against areas to create little dents which may then be textured with stone or discs.

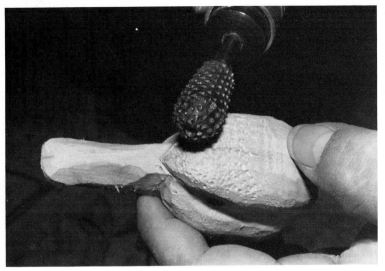

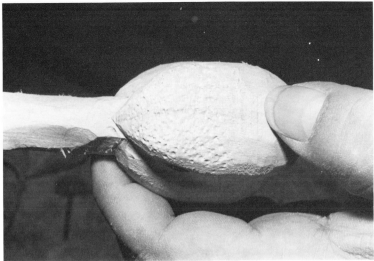

A. Example of solid rasp beating against head.

B. Example of head after beating.

C. Same area being textured with discs.

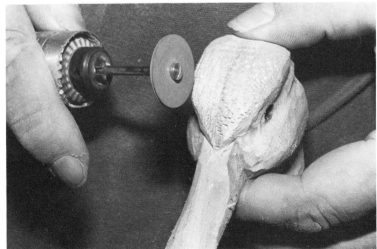

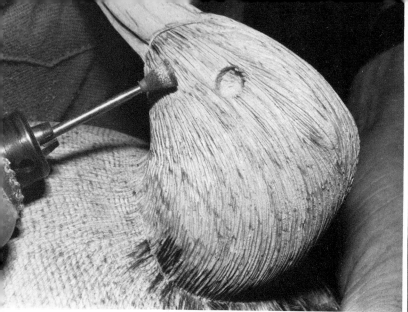

A. Example of a miniature canvasback head being textured with stone.

B. Example same as letter A.

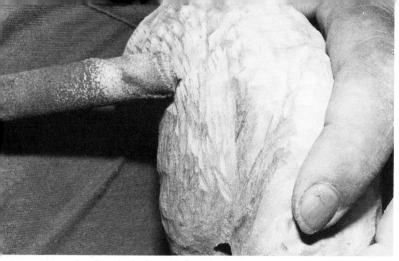

A. Example of a Red Head head being rough textured with coarse cartridge roll (tootsie roll).

B. Example of Red Head head using same procedure as A on back of crown.

C. Example of Red Head head using same procedure as A on cheek area (these areas are then generally fine textured with stone or burning pen or may be left as is.

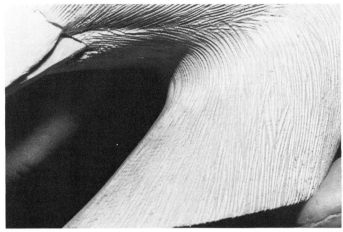

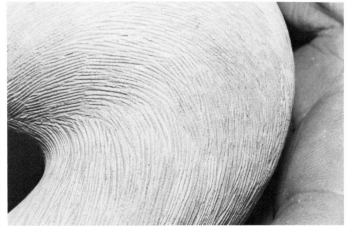

A. Example of Pintail neck textured with dental discs.

C. Example of Pintail cheek textured with dental discs. Note burned crown.

B. Example of Pintail cheek and neck textured with dental discs.

D. Example of Pintail back of neck textured with dental discs.

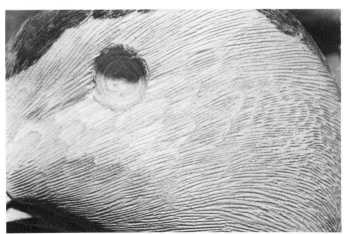

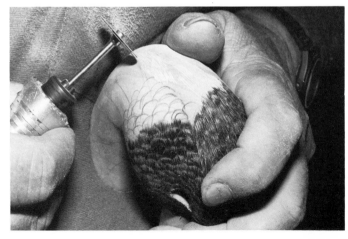

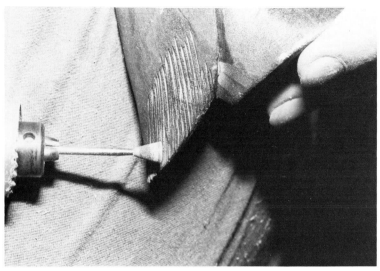

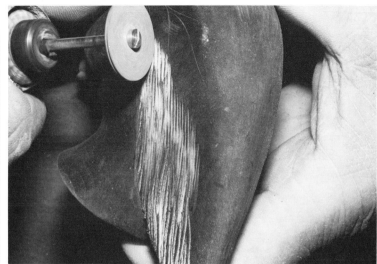

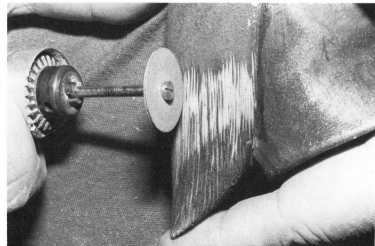

A. Example of rough texture with stone on Woody crest.

B. & C. Example of finer texturing on crest with dental discs.

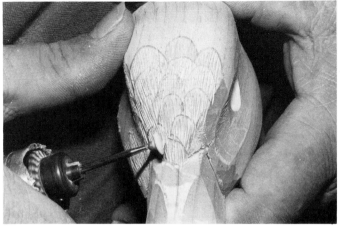

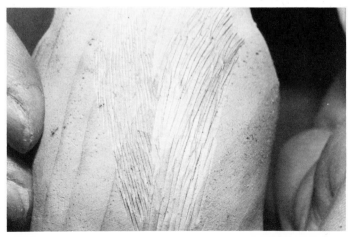

A. Example of feather pattern texturing with fine white stones.

C. Example of fine texturing on back of neck in a straight line.

B. Close up example of feather pattern texturing with fine white stones.

D. Example of coarse texturing on back of neck in a straight line.

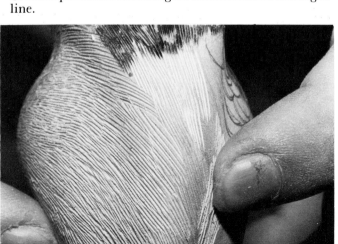

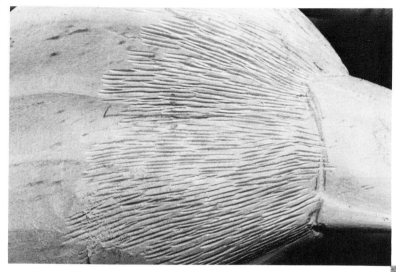

A. Example of fine texturing on cheek area of Mallard.

B. Example of coarse texturing under tail of Pintail.

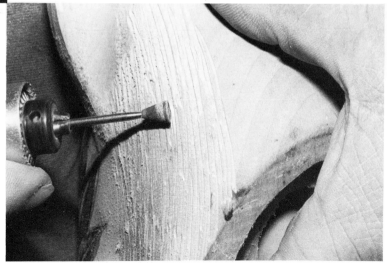

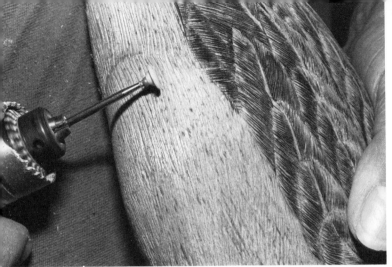

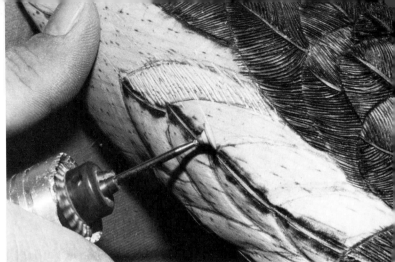

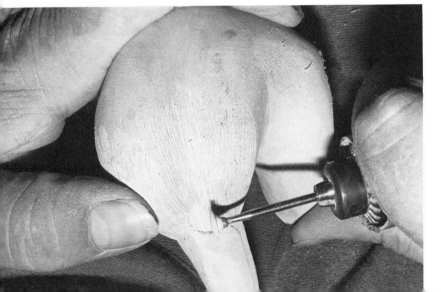

A. Example of fine texturing with stone on side pockets. Note burned back.

B. Example of fine texturing of underside of feather on side of Mallard hen.

C. Example of fine texturing on cheek of Teal hen head.

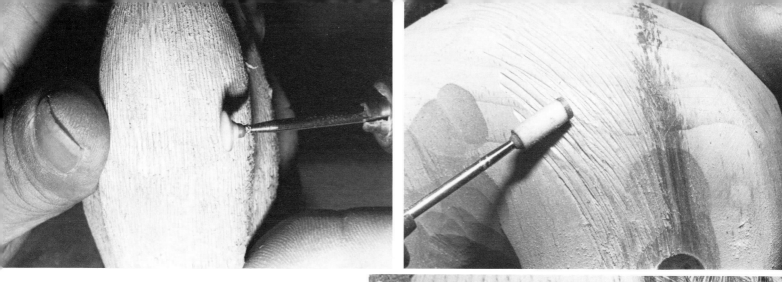

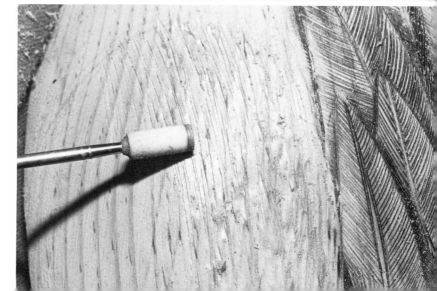

A. Example of fine texturing on crown of wood duck drake.

B. Example of coarse texturing on cheek of Mallard.

C. Coarse texturing on side of miniature canvasback.

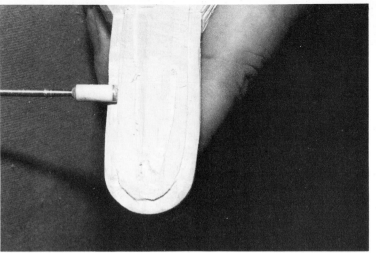

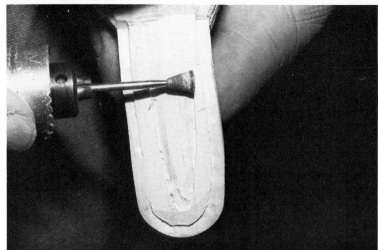

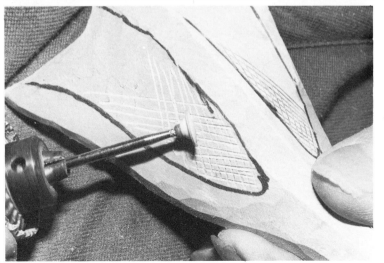

A. Use of white cylindrical stone to carve detail of underside of bill.

B. Use of reverse taper to carve underside of bill.

C. Use of small white stone to texture webs of feet.